THE GOLDILOCKS ZONE

A SHORT STORY

INCLUDED IN 'YOUR MOTHER'S NIGHTMARES', A
COLLECTION OF SIX TROUBLING TALES

ANITHA KRISHNAN

DREAM PEDLAR BOOKS

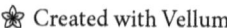 Created with Vellum

For Dhruv,
the greatest miracle in my life.
Thank you for showing me the difference between loneliness and
solitude. It is from you that I've learnt to summon the courage to
transcend one and embrace the other.

ABOUT THIS BOOK

The Goldilocks Zone

Newly suburban mother, Sonia, yearns for the support of a community to raise her almost three-year-old son, Aarash.

But she discovers, to her great disappointment, that her new neighbourhood is filled with far too many gestures of polite friendliness but no real friendship.

Until one day a bike accident transports them into a parallel world that promises her the perfect community she has been longing for.

But being part of a community means her child will no longer be only hers. Will she be willing to make such a sacrifice?

BEFORE WE BEGIN

Dear Reader,

Motherhood, or even parenting in general, is one of those life experiences that are almost universal yet remarkably unique to each one of us.

Everyone's parenting journey is vastly different. What works for one parent/family may simply not work for another.

My own journey has been a mix of unimaginable joys and unbelievable anxieties and everything else in between these two extremes.

During those dark moments, I turned to writing as a salve. I couldn't bring myself to speak aloud the fears I had for my child. Already wracked with anxiety and a deep sense of wrongness for even having those fears in the first place, I was terrified that putting them in written or spoken form—by journalling or talking about them to someone—might just make them come true.

Instead, I couched them in the guise of speculative fiction to render them more palatable, more surmountable, and as a reminder that in those moments my fears were exactly that—fiction!

It's for this very reason that I crafted the short story collection, *Your Mother's Nightmares*, a few months ago. *The Goldilocks Zone* is a short story from that six-tale collection.

If you're a parent, my hope is that in these pages, you too will find the words for the darkness you already know so intimately and grapple with every single day, and emerge into the light on the other side, feeling seen and sane and safe in the knowledge that you are doing the best you can and that is more than enough.

~ Anitha Krishnan
Burlington, Ontario,
Saturday, 22 June 2024

THE GOLDILOCKS ZONE

1

*I*t doesn't take me long to get used to riding the bakfiets. The basket bike. Aarash is admirably patient while I take the bike for a spin in the vast and mostly empty parking lot behind the bike shop.

My test-ride lasts less than five minutes, for most of which the sound of a child's cries keeps ringing in my ears. I decide I can learn on the go and return to the shop, confident of getting the hang of riding the beast sooner than later.

Aarash is waiting happily by the entrance in a blue helmet with Thomas The Tank Engine, Percy, and James grinning from the top of his head.

"Look what I chose," he leaps up at the sight of me and points to his helmet.

"Thomas!" I squeal with equal excitement.

"And Percy and James," he adds.

"You look like you're all set to go on a bike ride."

Aarash's face falls. "Not now," he shrugs. "Maybe later."

"How was the ride?" Nikhil squeezes my hand.

"Was he okay?" I ask Nikhil.

"Yah! He was having fun. Tell me, how was the ride?"

"Great!" I say. "Another practice ride, and I should be good to ride with Aarash."

Aarash, our only child, has a name that means the first ray of the sun. He is thirty-four months old. Not yet three years old. No longer two-and-a-half.

2

There is a series of moments I wait for every morning.

After we've had breakfast and Nikhil has left for work, Aarash climbs into the basket of the bakfiets, and we set out.

First, along Belvenia Road, past 4026, the home of Johann and Nataliya, our elderly Yugoslavian neighbours.

Then past 4050 Belvenia Road, where a tall ginger cat is perched inside the window, watching us with the kind of relaxed alertness that every human being in the world today aspires to achieve.

"I want to go there," Aarash once said, pointing to the cat.

"I know, sweetie, I would love to go meet that cat too." First, validate. Empathize. And then only reason. "But that is not our house. We can't just walk in there," I replied.

He thought for a moment, watching the cat with the kind of relaxed thoughtfulness that every grown-up desires to reclaim.

"Goldilocks!" he declared.

It took me a moment to first make the connection, and

then a second moment to marvel at the fact that my toddler had concocted such an incongruous link between a ginger cat and a fairy-tale heroine, and yet another moment to loudly laud his observation, and a final fourth moment to silently congratulate myself on this unexpected instance of motherly pride.

Up we continue now along Belvenia Road, past the bus stop in front of 4100, an apartment community for the elderly. I look for a familiar face in the row of first-floor balconies. An 86-year-old lady who walks her dog and always stops for a brief chat. I see her and we wave. I know her dog's name. Tanner. I don't know hers. I worry that when she dies, it will take me a very long time and a new tenant in her balcony to find out.

"I'd love a ride in that basket," another familiar voice hollers. It belongs to a plump, old lady with a jolly face who lives in one of the ground-floor apartments and is almost always in her tiny front yard, chatting with someone or the other. The very sight of her cheers me up.

"You can wait for your turn," Aarash reminds her. He's a real hoot.

And on we go and turn left onto the bike path, the Centennial Bikeway. And this is when I invariably tell myself I love Burlington. The city in Ontario, I mean. I have never set foot in its more popular namesake in Vermont. On the other side of the border.

We moved here a year ago from Toronto. From a one-bed condo in North York, to be more precise. A half-hour subway ride away from downtown Toronto.

When Hansal, an old friend of ours visited us from

London, UK (not to be confused with London, Ontario), he looked around and asked, "Have you ever played SimCity?"

Nikhil nodded, and I shook my head.

"Toronto looks like that," he explained. "A patchwork of random buildings built by amateur video game players. No character. No history. No vision." Well, obviously, it doesn't hold a candle to the UK.

But Burlington? I already love it here. What's not to love about a city where you are only a stone's throw away from the beach? Where it is legal to ride your bike on the sidewalk? What's not to love above a city that has a dedicated bike trail running through its heart and by the shoreline?

Don't move, my well-meaning friends in the city had warned us. "You," one of them had pointed a finger at me and said, "don't even have a license. You'll never survive in the burbs."

Look at me now. Suburban mom of one. Bike-rider. Eco-friendly. Making do with what I have.

The bike path winds past brambles and hedged backyards. An occasional rabbit skitters past. Robins and blackbirds swoop and soar. A tiny bridge leads us over a gentle stream, and we stop to watch a family of ducks, just sitting and doing nothing else at all.

We've had a very wet spring, so much so that the local beach has not yet opened for the season. But Burlington has been parched for a week now.

The sky is blue, the clouds are white, the sun is pleasantly warm. Lunch is packed and stowed under the seat alongside another bag carrying diapers, wipes and a change of clothes, and an entire day lies ahead of us for the taking, a day that seems to have spilled out of one of Enid Blyton's Famous Five books, brimming with adventure and fun.

"What is behind the sky?" Aarash asks.

I look up, my heart soaring at the kind of questions he conjures up while also sinking a little at the thought of the kind of answers I'll have to concoct. How does one even begin to attempt an answer to such a question?

"Maybe more sky?" I ask in return.

"Maybe," he nods, and relapses into silence.

I bought the bakfiets for the joy of conversation with my child sitting right in front of me rather than discarded and forgotten in a rear trailer, out of sight, out of mind.

Yet, our rides have transpired in silence more often than in conversation. The concoction of summer sun, the gentle bumpiness of the ride, and the buzz of katydids and cicadas often lull him to sleep.

We brake to a halt at the traffic lights at Cumberland Avenue. Just on the other side of the street, where the bike path resumes, is a steep, downhill slope that takes us down faster than any slide Aarash has been on.

And here it is. The moment we both wait for.

"Look what's coming up!" I holler, as the light turns green and I push forth, cranking the gears up and riding faster.

"Woohoo," I scream as the bike hurtles down the slope, preparing to splash through an unexpected puddle that Aarash spots at the bottom.

This is the moment I wait for each day.

The moment of free fall.

The moment in which I don't have to think about what to cook for our next meal or try to remember if it has been too long since the last diaper change.

The moment in which I don't worry about whether my little one will grow up and fall into prison or prostitution.

The moment when it ceases to matter that I've been unemployed for the last few years and we don't have enough money to go on vacation because the sun and the sky and the breeze of all of the world are right here, encapsulating my little one and me and our bike in an inexplicable bubble of happiness.

This is the moment in which I understand that parenting is all about wondering which will explode first: my head or my heart.

Turns out the answer is my head.

3

*L*ater, as I try to conjure up a memory of the crash, my first on the bakfiets, I will slot the events into a sequence that will reek of logic.

Aarash and I will talk about it over and over again, concoct a story from a memory, until he is reassured that an accident doesn't have to mean the end of our carefree rides down the bike path.

Right now, though, a number of things happen at once.

An abrupt flash of pink and grey.

A swerve and a thud.

A loud hiss and a meow.

A screech and a groaning scrape.

The ground turning sky blue. The sky turning concrete grey and grass green.

Aarash slip-sliding out of sight.

Terror paralyzing my throat and jaws.

No opportunity to scream.

Vision consumed by blackness.

4

"Wake up, Mumma, it's morning!"
Tiny lips press upon my cheek.

"Thank you, precious." I hug my child, keeping my eyes squeezed shut, hoping to cuddle with him for a few more minutes of sleep. Aarash has other plans.

"Look where we are!" He shakes my shoulders as something soft and cold and wet shifts swiftly under me.

I open my eyes and the first thing I see is Aarash's beautiful face stretched into a grin. Behind him is the vast sky and a warm, distant sun.

I sit up.

Under and all around us are sand and water and horizon as far as the eye can see. The water is cool and light. No smell of salt in the air. Lake Ontario, most likely. Has the Burlington beach been opened for the season?

A bunch of children splash about in the water near us. People I may or may not have seen before but can't quite place are sprawled on beach mats or loungers, reading books or doing nothing.

I look behind and find the bakfiets parked there, our lunch and diaper bag still miraculously stowed under the basket seat atop which now lies a pale pink Canadian Sphynx, curled in a Fibonacci spiral.

I know nothing about cats. It just so happens that our neighbour Cindy at 4020 Belvenia Road owns a dog and two cats, one of which is a Canadian Sphynx, nine months old. I wonder if the creature sprawled in our bakfiets is Cindy's.

"We're at the beach," Aarash jumps up. "Summer is here!"

He leaps into the waves and runs toward a group of three- and four-year-olds, frolicking in the water.

This is not Aarash, I think as I look at him. Aarash is quite like Nikhil, watchful, cautious at first in any new situation.

I am the one who throws caution to the wind, confident of figuring it out as we go. Okay, correction. I *was* the one who *used to throw* caution to the wind.

I am a different person now, the kind that feels anxious and worries that something is amiss at the sight of her usually reticent toddler playing with a bunch of unfamiliar peers on an unknown beach.

Thankfully, I know when not to complain. I can't remember the last time I was not needed by Aarash, and so I take this moment to watch my child lose himself in play. It is quite meditative.

Something velvety brushes against my arm from behind, and the naked, fur-free, velvety Sphynx makes her way to a spot beside me. She looks at me with eyes yellow like the distant sun.

I wonder if she is asking to be petted. Where I come from, that great land of myths and spirits on the other side of the world, I'd be deemed a grave sinner if even a single hair from the body of a cat were to fall to the ground on account of me. Even an offering in gold weighing more than the cat, now missing a strand of hair, made to Lord Shiva, the Great God of Destruction, would not relieve me of the burden of my sin for eternity. Or so I was warned in my younger days by grown-ups, well-intentioned no doubt.

I look up and see Aarash throwing occasional glances my way in the midst of his play with his newfound friends. That strange child, who watches me more closely than any God does. I must think of the examples I am setting for him. Besides, Canadian Sphynxes surely have no hair.

I reach out to stroke her under her chin but before I can, she transforms into my animal-loving, red-haired neighbour, Cindy, dressed in yoga pants and stretching into a graceful Marjaryasana, looking like a 60s celebrity.

"Surprise!" She grins at me.

"Cindy!" I yell, pulling back my hand. "Surprise, indeed! Though shock would have been a more apt word. What are you doing here?"

"Waiting for you, Sonia," Cindy replies, as she sits comfortably beside me. "And I've been waiting for a very long time. Most mothers end up here even before their first-borns turn one."

And just like that, I feel like an instant failure again, anxious that I have committed some irreversible mistakes on this parenting journey that will scar Aarash forever.

"Where are we?" I ask.

Cindy gets up. "Let's go for a walk," she says, and I follow.

I need to tell Aarash where I am headed but he is out of earshot, so I wave my hands to get his attention.

"He'll be fine," Cindy assures me, and a part of me wants to believe her but a bigger part of me won't allow it. Surprisingly, I quell my fear for once and walk.

"Let's not go too far then," I say. "What is this place anyway?"

"Welcome to the Goldilocks Zone!" Cindy announces.

"It sure looks like we are in the midst of a fairy tale," I chuckle.

Cindy looks a little alarmed. "You do know what a Goldilocks Zone is, don't you?"

"Hmm ... not really," I admit. "I hope we won't run into any hungry bears though." Stop talking, I tell myself, before I reveal any more of my ignorance.

"A Goldilocks Zone is a place where everything is just right," Cindy explains. "It is usually used in the context of stars. It is the area around a star where it is neither too hot nor too cold, and the temperature is just right for liquid water to exist on any planet in that zone. And where water exists, so does life."

"Like on Earth," I say, eager as a student willing to learn and understand.

"Exactly. Now let's take that concept and apply it to our lives. Don't you wish your life conditions felt just right? Not too rushed yet not too slow? Not too much nor too little to do? Especially with a little child to look after?"

I want to let myself break apart right here and now and tell Cindy everything about what a delightful child Aarash is yet how hard it is to care for a little one.

How there are days when I look at the poetry that he is and realize that watching him play is the best form of meditation I have come across.

And yet there are days when time seems to have come to a

standstill, but somehow, I continue to fall into an endless abyss, and I think this is it, I will not survive this day to see the sun set and rise yet again.

But I don't. I don't tell Cindy any of this because I don't want her to call Social Services on me.

Now, I am not being paranoid. As a mom, the first thing I realized was that people are always watching and judging your every move, though very rarely in your favour. Wasn't it only last week that a nosy neighbour in Hamilton reported a mother for letting her three-year-old play in their fenced backyard, unsupervised?

So, I throw my head back and laugh instead. A hearty, confident laugh that I ardently hope will belie my absolute ineptitude at playing mom. "With a child, there's always too much to do and too little that gets done," I say. "Either everything's happening all at once or nothing is happening at all. But it doesn't feel wrong. You get what I mean? All the messiness. The sleeplessness. The inadequacy of it all. The ordinariness of it all. Isn't that what it's supposed to be?"

"That is what the world will have you believe, m'dear." Cindy is ecstatic, as if I have unwittingly steered the conversation in the direction she was aiming for. "The truth is … and bear in mind, this truth has been hidden from mothers, from women, for aeons. Motherhood doesn't have to be messy or inadequate or ordinary. You do not have to be sleep-deprived. The truth is, your child, he is not *your* burden alone to bear."

The truth always stings. I feel myself burning up from within, my stomach churning, my face growing hot, my nose and lungs refusing to help me breathe, even as the cool breeze whips my unwashed, but mercifully short, hair about my face.

The sun remains bleak in the distance, and the water cool beneath our feet.

I stop walking and look around to check on Aarash. My incredibly delightful child. Not even in my darkest hours have I deemed him a *burden*.

More children have joined the group he is with. Taller, bigger ones with surprisingly great observation skills yet very little awareness of the world immediately around them. They are roughhousing, and Aarash is standing on the fringes, watching, as he always does.

"He'll be fine," Cindy says and nudges me to continue walking.

But I don't feel fine. I feel anger and caution and anxiety all bubbling up from somewhere deep inside of me, a dormant volcano waking up, ready to jolt the world from its oblivion, its disregard.

"So, whose burden is he then?"

"Every child is the responsibility of the entire community," Cindy says. "You know the old adage … it takes a village. And that is what makes this place perfect. Just right. Everybody pitches in. You help care for a bunch of children when you can, and their mothers help look after Aarash. How much time do you get to yourself these days? An hour? Or two? Imagine what you can do with eight, ten hours of child-free time on your hand each day. All the poetry you can write, the stories you can read, the songs you can sing, the worlds you can change. All that without having to lose any sleep ever again."

5

*D*o you remember I told you about Hansal? That old friend of ours who visited us from London, UK (not to be confused with London, Ontario)? The one who likened Toronto to a SimCity development?

Aarash was not even a year old when Hansal visited us. I remember telling him I wish I had forty-eight hours in a day. Twenty-four to devote to the care of Aarash. And twenty-four to live the life I'd had before Aarash, and all the lives I'd have lived had he not turned up unexpectedly in my womb more than three years ago.

"It is a tough choice," Hansal had said back then. "An impossible choice."

Cindy makes a compelling argument. Which new mom wouldn't want more time, more child-free time to devote to matters that have nothing to do with her child or her home?

It makes sense now, what Cindy said earlier, about me being late, about other mothers turning up here in this picture-perfect, just-right Goldilocks Zone even before their infants turn one, willing to sacrifice the individualities of their children at the altar of community.

But I will not be fooled for an instant into believing that another person could ever love my child as her own.

Truth be told, I've never had much love for children in the first place. I love Aarash with as much ferocity as gentleness, but it is as if the intensity with which I feel for him has left me even more indifferent to his peers. I have certainly no contribution to make to this system of communal caregiving.

And I shudder to think of the consequences that Aarash may be made to face for my inability to coo over and care for another's child as my own.

"There must be a huge price to pay for such a gift?" I ask.

Cindy is silent for a moment but to her credit, she says, truthfully, (or so I think), "No mother has asked that question in over a hundred years now."

"Perhaps they were too tired to think," I say, letting the sarcasm creep into my voice.

"Yes." Cindy nods. "But to answer your question, there is indeed a price to pay. Not everyone considers it to be astronomical though."

"What is it?"

"Right now," Cindy begins, "all you can think of are all the things you could do if only you had a little more time, a little more sleep, a little more energy. Most of your thoughts are of all the lives you think you can have if only you had a little more help with Aarash. When you leave him in another's care for the first time, your head will swell with thoughts only of him. And everything else will cease to exist. All the stories and songs and poetry of this world will no longer be alluring in his absence."

"Why on earth …?" I open my mouth to protest the glaring preposterousness of her proposition, but Cindy holds her hand up and raises her eyebrows and I am stalled.

"It will take you a while to find meaning again in a life in which Aarash is not eternally present. How long? That depends entirely on you. Mothers who join us earlier take no longer than a week. Two, at most. You've waited far too long to join us. It will take you longer. It will be harder for you. But the more you delay, the more difficult it will be."

It doesn't take me long to see the dichotomy of it all. Even as I wonder if all the decisions I've made until now have led me and Aarash and Nikhil down a horribly wrong path, something tells me I need to trust myself a little more. I look at Aarash for an answer.

This gentle child, moving through this world at his own pace, unperturbed by all the noise and frenzy around him, already at home in this world where countless others are miserable and lost even after decades of existence. He stands out like the first ray of sunshine in the morning.

Who am I to tear him apart from his true self now only so that he can grow up to haunt the corners of this world like a lost soul, searching for the very home he was pushed out of as a child?

And for what? For more time for me? For more Aarash-free time? For more time for me to deny the existence of this child who is more exquisite than poetry, whose voice is the melody of this Universe, who is a completely unpredictable story unfurling right in front of my very eyes every day, every moment, and who has changed my world in ways I didn't even know was possible?

Whom I deem a blessing is a burden to another. What I

believe is a huge price to pay, the absence of my child, is another's idea of a gift, a rare privilege.

"And what about Aarash?" I keep coming back to the same question in every situation. What about Aarash?

"What about him?"

"How long will it take him to adjust to this new arrangement?"

"Look at him." Cindy shrugs. "He has already adapted."

The group of children has grown so large it is a darned crowd out there, and I struggle to find Aarash at first. But there he is, waist deep in water, jumping right into a big, frothy wave that crashes down upon him.

"Children can be quite resilient, if only we can trust them to be," Cindy says with finality.

Suddenly I feel an acute sense of absence, an Aarash-shaped hole that I know not what to fill with.

What if Cindy is right? What if it is too late? Who am I without Aarash? Who will I be when Aarash grows up and won't need me any longer?

But does that mean I should abandon him now when he still needs me?

True, he has been playing for the last half hour or so without calling out to me. An unexpected first for him. But how much of this development is because of being in the Goldilocks Zone and how much of it is age-appropriate behaviour?

And then it strikes me. Sure, Goldilocks found all the things that were just right for her. But what about the bears?

The story ends with three hungry bears, deprived of a homemade meal and left with a broken chair and ruffled beds to deal with. Someone always has to pay a price.

All along we've been deluding ourselves that it is the mothers who have been making the greatest sacrifices.

But the ones who truly suffer in all this charade are the children.

The infants, who are expected to sleep through the night so that their parents can sleep, undisturbed.

The toddlers, who are expected to keep themselves engaged so that their parents can take a cell phone break.

The pre-schoolers, who are expected to demonstrate emotional restraint, a feat that most grown-ups have rarely aspired to, let alone achieved.

All the children, who are resented for simply being children in a world of adults. They are the ones who pay the price.

I have a sudden desire to get away from Cindy, from this stupid place with all its illusion of everything being 'just right'. For that is what it is. An illusion.

Because wanting to have it all is akin to wanting to have nothing at all.

The desire for forty-eight hours in a day devalues the twenty-four that exist, ripe for the taking. In the absence of the four dozen hours I want, I spend the two dozen that I have moaning about the other two dozen that I don't have.

What a laugh!

When we want everything, we get nothing.

Everything becomes nothing.

All becomes none.

Voila! I have concocted my own koan, I muse.

The realization of this makes me suddenly giddy. I have a sudden urge to fly, my spirit is soaring, but my body is at first too heavy to be lifted into transcendence.

And then, I let go. I let go of all the ideas and notions of how everything should be and bask in the delicate impermanence of this moment in which Aarash and I exist, safe and happy.

I am flying now, over to Aarash. Cindy and her sermons are a distant memory. I am free at last, free from the opinions and judgements of others as well as from my own doubts and anxieties. Perhaps, this is what enlightenment is.

"Mumma," I hear Aarash call out to me, the sound of his voice lifting me like the wind I am sailing on.

"Coming, precious," I call out, as I glide towards him.

An arm shoots out from his vicinity and shoves him into the water. And just like that, Aarash disappears.

"Noooo!" I scream and swoop down on the murderous arm and snap it into two.

Shrieks and cries erupt as if there were three million, and not merely three dozen, people on the beach.

I duck underwater to look for Aarash.

And all I see is a black, bottomless pit.

All I hear is an angry roar.

And the last thing I recall is my own inner voice cursing me for not having signed up for swimming lessons yet again.

6

"**Mumma**," Aarash's voice snaps me out of my reverie.

"What, cutie?" I ask. I am a little giddy as if I've travelled a great distance too fast and haven't yet had a chance to catch my breath.

"Green light," he says.

And here we are again. At the traffic lights at Cumberland Avenue. Across the street from where the bike path resumes, from that steep, downhill slope with the puddle through which we crashed into the Goldilocks Zone.

"Are you okay?" I ask Aarash, remembering him being held underwater by a child whose hand I had broken. "Who pushed you underwater?"

"When, Mumma?" Aarash asks.

"At the beach."

"You said the beach is still closed."

"Oh, right. It is, isn't it?"

When the light turns green again, I push forth reluctantly. We cross the street and are now at the top of the slope.

We've had a very wet spring and the lake has spilled over the narrow strip of beach where we spent most evenings last summer. It hasn't rained in over a week now. The beach remains closed but there is no puddle on the bike path.

"Woohoo," I scream as the bike hurtles down the slope.

This is the moment I wait for each day.

The moment of free fall.

The moment of rapidly changing perceptions.

Everything becomes nothing.

All becomes none.

This is the moment of knowing that a sacrifice to one may be a simple matter of choice to another.

And so, I choose. I choose to be with Aarash now, flying down this bike path that cuts through the heart of Burlington, the sun and the wind kissing our faces.

Look at Aarash, free to be himself, with no pressing need to lose himself first only to spend a lifetime retracing his path to his lost self.

Everything is already *just right*, right here, right now. Why do we need to ruin it and then spend this one life trying to make it *just right* all over again?

"*I* don't want to be a person. I want to be a cat," Aarash says at breakfast and proceeds to lick the scrambled eggs off his plate.

It is already tomorrow here in Belvenia Road. It always astounds me how the days fly by and crawl at the same time. My little one is not so little anymore. He is beginning to have aspirations now.

"What do you like about being a cat?" I ask.

"Hmm ... I just like being a cat."

"I wonder if cats like going to the beach. What do you think?"

"You were walking with a cat the other day at the beach," he reminds me.

"Which cat? Which other day?"

"One day, a very long time ago, Mumma, Aarash, and Cindy went to the beach." Aarash turns storyteller now. So here comes a dramatic pause.

"And then what happened?"

"All three of us played in the water together. And we had a lot of fun. The end."

"That sounds swell," I say. "Would you like Cindy to come to the beach with us one day? Maybe we could ask her."

"Of course!" Aarash hops off his chair and proceeds to grab his slippers.

"Now?"

"Yes, let's go, Mumma!" He pulls his slippers on, places my pair by the door, and waits for me.

"Okay." I try to sound more enthused than alarmed by this sudden urge for socialization that my nearly-three-year-old is exhibiting.

"And maybe, she can tell me how to become a cat," Aarash muses.

~

Ready for more fantasy short stories on the motherhood experience? Check out the collection, Your Mother's Nightmares: Six Troubling Tales, which includes five more twisted tales on the motherhood experience.

When you buy the collection directly from my store, please treat yourself to a 40% discount using the code YMN40.

Please note the code YMN40 is valid only for the short story collection — Your Mother's Nightmares: Six Troubling Tales — in ebook format when purchased directly from my PayHip store, Dream Pedlar Books.
Go to https://payhip.com/b/SfQvj to redeem your code!

ENJOYED THE GOLDILOCKS ZONE?

Thank you for reading *The Goldilocks Zone!*

If you loved the story, I hope you will consider writing a short review—even a simple line or two—on the site where you bought the book.

Publishing is still driven by word of mouth, and when you leave a review it helps other readers decide this is a story worth reading. Thank you for your help in spreading the word.

You can also sign up to my monthly newsletter for updates on new book releases as well as heartfelt reflections on writing, reading, parenting and living the creative life.

Monthly Missives from The Dream Pedlar
https://thedreampedlar.com/newsletter

AUTHOR'S NOTE

Dear Reader,

Unlike many other stories I've written, I remember exactly what inspired me to write *The Goldilocks Zone*.

You see, we've spent much of the early childhood of our child, D (Dhruv), in solitude. It was the three of us, my husband Abhinav, D and me, for the most part, what with family being so far away in India.

I used to be on several parenting groups on FaceBook, and one constant refrain was that parenting in a nuclear family setup is impossible. What we all need is a community.

I've often fantasized having a large, multi-generational family, like the ones in books and movies, where everyone looks out for each other and has each other's backs, where you know you have people you can trust and reach out to when in need.

But often we forget that these other members of this so-called 'community' are people too. People with their own opinions and beliefs, especially when it comes to raising a child. People who have expectations of us just as we too have some expectations of them in terms of behaviours and attitudes. People with whom we have relationships that need to be cultivated and managed alongside the already difficult task of parenting.

Living in a community may not be as easy and hunky-dory as we imagine it to be, especially when we're struggling with looking after a small child and any alternative to doing it all by ourselves comes across as a tempting cure-all.

I used to listen to meditation teacher Tara Brach's talks a lot in those days. One anecdote she often shared was the story of a group of porcupines, each of whom was shivering in the cold. Then they huddled together for warmth, and that indeed proved to be a successful strategy in keeping the cold at bay, except that each was inadvertently poked by the others' quills.

In essence, when we seek the warmth and support of a community, we are also vulnerable to the hurts and wounds that inevitably come from two or more people living together or in constant, close contact with each other.

I shied away from seeking much help in those days; I was in a very vulnerable state of mind, very sensitive to judgement, and I was looking for the perfect kind of support in which I'd be helped but not judged.

Maybe that was asking for too much, and in a way I too was judging the other.

Well-meaning friends would ask me to come over and watch a movie, when all I really wanted back then in those early days was to be with little D.

Talking about parenting woes with other moms sometimes ended up becoming like a competitive sport; the medal goes to whoever could prove they have it harder.

Many well-intentioned folks would give us advice with the

expectation that we'd follow it; they'd feel insulted if we chose to not act on their suggestion.

The number of people who told me that I ought to put D in daycare was far too many to keep track of; it added to my guilt of choosing to be a stay-at-home mom to him.

I knew even back then, and I can say so with much confidence even now, that the child thrived and continues to thrive on having free, unstructured time. But constantly being told to make choices other than the ones I was making significantly eroded my self-trust and confidence in my ability to parent well.

My parents and Abhinav poured unconditional love on me in those days. Somehow they knew how to give me space even when I myself didn't know how to ask for it gracefully. They knew how to listen without offering advice or judgement, understanding that sometimes I just needed to talk things out loud to make sense of it all.

These are invaluable qualities they possess, and now I too try to show up in that way for the people I meet in the course of my day-to-day life.

This is really a tricky balance to find. Those FaceBook parenting groups formed my community in those days. I could spend time there as and when I needed, and switch off when I wanted space and silence.

We can't have these on-off switches when other people are involved in real life. They are human, not a random website on the Internet that we can shut off when we've had our fill.

I think of the story of porcupines a lot to help keep things in perspective when we are with extended family.

It also helps to remember that even in a nuclear family, our quills do end up poking the others and vice versa on occasion.

And finally, it really helps to remember that the Goldilocks Zone is most certainly an illusion, at least when it comes to parenting and life in general. There is no perfect way. There is no easy way. It's a very difficult task.

The best we can do is to make the most of the situation we're in, instead of wishing we had more family or less, instead of believing that the grass is greener on the other side. Life, after all, is truly not about what happens to us but about how we respond to it.

Thank you for reading this far. I'd love to stay in touch with you. And I hope you'd like to stay connected with me too.

I send out a monthly newsletter on the last Sunday of every month filled with heartfelt musings on the joys of writing, reading and living the creative life. Subscription is free.

You will be the first to hear of my forthcoming works. I also include updates on my writing life, book recommendations, free short fiction, and occasional surprises.

Thank you for staying with me this far. If you choose to accompany me further on this journey, I promise you a magical ride.

Climb aboard at https://thedreampedlar.com/newsletter!

~ Anitha Krishnan
Burlington, Ontario
Saturday, 22 June 2024

MORE BOOKS BY ANITHA KRISHNAN

https://thedreampedlar.com/books/

Dying Wishes

Finalist, 2023 Rakuten Kobo Emerging Writer Prize in Speculative Fiction

A contemporary fantasy novel weaving Hindu mythology and South Indian folklore into a quest for belonging across different worlds — the World of Mortals and the World of Gods, India and Canada, the past and the present, the world outside and the one within.

Erased from Existence

A paranormal mystery in which a fifteen-year-old is erased from the memories and perception of everyone. Trapped in oblivion, she will have to unearth and reveal long-buried family secrets to escape.

The Land of No Reflection

A fantasy tale of two sightless young women on the run from their homeland, having committed the unpardonable crime of seeing.

A Benevolent Goddess

A story of a goddess who is punished for her desire to help human beings but is unable to find salvation by any other means.

In Search of Leo

A fantasy tale exploring the gamut of emotions that loss and grief can stir.

The Mind Meddler

A short fantasy story on the games The Mind Meddler plays by sneaking thoughts into people's minds, until he meets the one person who can resist his unkind mischief.

Mrs. D'Souza's Dispute With God

A fantasy short story in which a school teacher, Mrs. D'Souza, dies unexpectedly and sets out in search of God to demand answers to her burning questions on life and death.

Hello, Dreamer! Poems & Dreams

An eclectic collection of 100 short poems encompassing musings on the universe and its mysteries, nature and human life, my secret longings and fears, love and heartbreak, the sun and the moon, the stars and the seas, light and shadow, and joy and nostalgia.

ABOUT THE AUTHOR

Anitha Krishnan is a speculative fiction author and an award-winning poet. Her fantasy novel, *Dying Wishes*, was a finalist for the 2023 Rakuten Kobo Emerging Writer Prize in the Speculative Fiction category.

She has lived in and left pieces of her heart in many places across the world including Singapore, Australia, Canada, and most of all in her beloved birthplace, India. She presently lives in Burlington, Ontario with her husband and their cherished child.

Find more books and her blog on the writing life at
https://thedreampedlar.com.

Sign up to her monthly newsletter at
https://thedreampedlar.com/newsletter
to receive heartfelt musings, exclusive updates, book
recommendations, free fiction, and more!